Giant Hornets

by Trudy Becker

FOCUS READERS®

PIONEER

www.focusreaders.com

Focus Readers is distributed by North Star Editions:
sales@northstareditions.com | 888-417-0195

Produced for Focus Readers by Red Line Editorial.

Photographs ©: iStockphoto, cover, 1, 6, 14, 17, 20; Shutterstock Images, 4, 8, 10; Karla Salp/Washington State Department of Agriculture/AP Images, 12; Scott Camazine/Science Source, 18

Library of Congress Cataloging-in-Publication Data
Names: Becker, Trudy, author.
Title: Giant hornets / Trudy Becker.
Description: Lake Elmo, MN : Focus Readers, [2023]. | Series: Bugs |
   Includes index. | Audience: Grades 2-3
Identifiers: LCCN 2022031726 (print) | LCCN 2022031727 (ebook) | ISBN
   9781637394502 (hardcover) | ISBN 9781637394878 (paperback) | ISBN
   9781637395608 (pdf) | ISBN 9781637395240 (ebook)
Subjects: LCSH: Vespa mandarinia--Juvenile literature.
Classification: LCC QL568.V5 B34 2023 (print) | LCC QL568.V5 (ebook) |
   DDC 595.79/8--dc23/eng/20220524
LC record available at https://lccn.loc.gov/2022031726
LC ebook record available at https://lccn.loc.gov/2022031727

Printed in the United States of America
Mankato, MN
012023

About the Author

Trudy Becker lives in Minneapolis, Minnesota. She likes exploring new places and loves anything involving books.

Table of Contents

Chapter 1

Deadly Attack

A giant hornet lands on a branch. It spots an insect nearby. Then it swoops down and attacks. The other insect has no chance. The giant hornet is too strong.

Giant hornets are the biggest hornets in the world. Their **habitats** are low forests and mountains. Most giant hornets live in China and Japan.

Fun Fact Some giant hornets live in North America. They first arrived in 2019.

Chapter 2

Big Bodies

Giant hornets have large yellow heads. Their bodies have black and yellow stripes. Giant hornets have big wings, too. The wings attach to the middle part of the body.

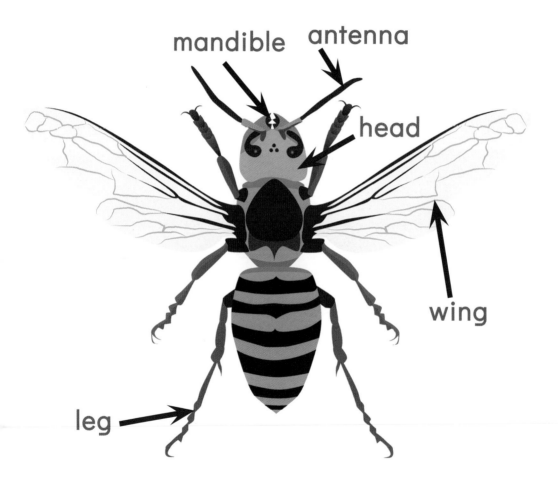

mandible antenna

head

wing

leg

Giant hornets are insects. So, they have six legs. They also have **mandibles**. Giant hornets use them to cut up their **prey**.

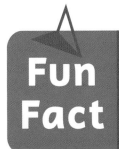

Fun Fact

Giant hornets can be up to 2 inches (5 cm) long.

stinger

Chapter 3

Giant Hornet Strengths

Some giant hornets have **stingers**. The stingers are smooth. Giant hornets can use them again and again. That helps giant hornets beat their prey.

The stingers have **venom**. This venom goes into giant hornets' prey. It hurts or kills them. The venom can even harm animals much bigger than giant hornets.

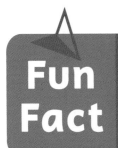

Fun Fact

Sometimes giant hornets are called "murder hornets."

Hive Attack

Sometimes giant hornets attack beehives. They cut off the bees' heads. The giant hornets can kill the whole hive. The attack can take just 90 minutes. After that, the giant hornets control the hive.

Chapter 4

Giant Hornet Life

Giant hornets eat insects. Sometimes they even eat other kinds of hornets. They eat beetles and bees, too. Giant hornets don't have many **predators**.

In spring, **queen** giant hornets make nests. They lay eggs. Workers feed and protect the group. They die in the fall. When spring returns, the queen lays new eggs.

Fun Fact Giant hornets usually make nests underground.

FOCUS ON
Giant Hornets

Write your answers on a separate piece of paper.

1. Write a sentence that explains the main idea of Chapter 2.

2. Would you want to see a giant hornet? Why or why not?

3. How do giant hornets use their mandibles?
   - A. They lift heavy pieces of food.
   - B. They use them to cut their prey.
   - C. They make sounds to scare predators.

4. Why don't giant hornets have many predators?
   - A. Animals don't want to eat giant hornets because they taste bad.
   - B. Giant hornets fly very fast, so other animals can't catch them.
   - C. Giant hornets' size, stinger, and mandibles make them too strong.

Answer key on page 24.

Glossary

habitats
Places where animals live.

mandibles
Jaws that stick out from an insect's head.

predators
Animals that hunt other animals for food.

prey
Animals that are eaten by other animals.

queen
A large female insect that lays the eggs for a colony.

stingers
Sharp body parts that can poke other animals and put poison into them.

venom
Poison that comes from an animal's sting or bite.

To Learn More

BOOKS

Hansen, Grace. *Asian Giant Hornet*. Minneapolis: Abdo Publishing, 2021.

Jaycox, Jaclyn. *Murder Hornets*. North Mankato, MN: Capstone Press, 2023.

NOTE TO EDUCATORS

Visit **www.focusreaders.com** to find lesson plans, activities, links, and other resources related to this title.

Index

Answer Key: **1.** Answers will vary; **2.** Answers will vary; **3.** B; **4.** C